FIRE *into* ICE

Adventures in Glass Making

by

James Houston

Tundra Books

Published in Canada by Tundra Books, *McClelland & Stewart Young Readers*,
481 University Avenue, Toronto, Ontario M5G 2E9

Published in the United States by Tundra Books of Northern New York,
P.O. Box 1030, Plattsburgh, New York 12901

Library of Congress Catalog Number: 98-60387

Canadian Cataloguing in Publication Data

Houston, James, 1921-
    Fire into ice: adventures in glass making

Includes index.
ISBN 0-88776-459-2

1. Steuben Glass, inc. – Juvenile literature. 2. Glass sculpture, American – New York (State) – Corning – Juvenile literature. 3. Glass manufacture – New York (State) – Corning – Juvenile literature. I. Title.

NK5198.S7H68 1998   j748.29147'83   C98-930697-6

We acknowledge the support of the Canada Council for the Arts for our publishing program.

We acknowledge the financial support of the Government of Canada through the Book Publishing Industry Development Program for our publishing activities.

Design: James Houston

Printed and bound in Spain
D.L. TO: 1015 - 1998

1 2 3 4 5 6   03 02 01 00 99 98

For Hart and Sam Houston,
my grandsons

A boy sat outside his father's tent in summer.
A mosquito came and landed on his arm.
The boy drew back his hand to strike.
"Don't hit! Don't hit!" the mosquito whined.
"I have many songs and stories yet
to sing to my grandchildren!"
"Imagine that," said the boy.
"You, so small, and yet a grandfather!"

An Inuit/Eskimo Myth

It was like white magic living inside an igloo, a snowhouse round and glistening, with an ice window and a stone seal-oil lamp for light and heat. During the 12 years I lived with Inuit/Eskimos, they taught me their ancient art of stone, bone, and ivory carving, and I taught them their newer art of stone block and stencil printing. Over those years, I lived with families gathered into small groups to hunt and travel and share food. They even taught me how to walk on thin ice.

An adventurer came into the Arctic in August 1959 and asked me to go south to design glass. Three years later, I felt I had completed my work in the Far North and agreed to go to New York because I delight in creating different art forms and living in new places. It was hard to leave those kind and clever Inuit/Eskimo people who had been my friends for so long.

I gave away my dog team and sled, my rifles, sleeping bag and parkas. After shaking hands with everyone, even the smallest babies riding in their mothers' hoods, I started out over the snow-covered ice. That was in May 1962, when it stayed light all night. I went with one of the Royal Canadian Mounted Police across Baffin Island to Iqaluit, then boarded a plane that carried me south.

Getting off the plane in New York seemed like stepping inside an oven packed with rushing, sweating crowds. Arthur A. Houghton, Jr., the man who had bet that I wouldn't stay to be a glassmaker, drove me to his house in mid-Manhattan. His wife showed me their guest room where I struggled out of my thick clothes, took a long ice-cold shower, and went down to dinner. Later that night, I returned upstairs. Listening to the wail of fire engine and police car sirens, I looked out at the thousands of lighted windows, sparkling like modern castles high in the starless sky. Already I was missing the lonesome singing of my husky dogs and the ghostly greenish curtains of the northern lights above.

The next day, everyone at the Steuben building welcomed me warmly. Other designers asked me to lunch, and the Houghtons took me to dinner. The very good but too-rich food in the best restaurants became my problem. Instead of half frozen fish and wild red meat, which I had learned to enjoy, the New York menus offered heavily-oiled green salads, sticky creamed chicken, and lemon meringue pie. It was tame food, but I pretended to like it. Later that night, I had dreams about polar bears.

I was missing the arctic families and animals and birds that I had known so well. I longed for the cold, clean, open country that I admired so much. I had visions of seals plunging into the icy depths.

Glass making is a very old and unique art that is said to have started in Persia about 3,000 years ago.

Unlike other artists and craftspeople, glassmakers rarely work alone. Artisans in glass combine the efforts of several people. The old European glassmakers were often helped by their wives and children, who heaped the glass furnaces first with charcoal, then hardwood branches. When the glass got hot and melted, the gaffer – the head of the glassworkers' team – would gather it on the end of a long iron, then finish shaping the glass before burying it in sand to allow it to cool.

Steuben glass is made of sand, ash, lead, and cullet – old glass – to give its clear crystal a special brilliance. It is heavy and reflects light beautifully.

Glass may be blown or shaped and fire polished when it is very hot: 2,500 degrees Fahrenheit, five times hotter than a household oven. Later, glass may be cut, after it has become as hard as ice. When glass is cold, it may be ground smooth, or frosted, or engraved using a copper wheel. Most sculptures we make are about the size of an adult's outstretched hand.

If a piece of our glass is judged to be good, it is signed with a diamond point. If it is less than perfect, it is smashed into a barrel and the broken glass is sold.

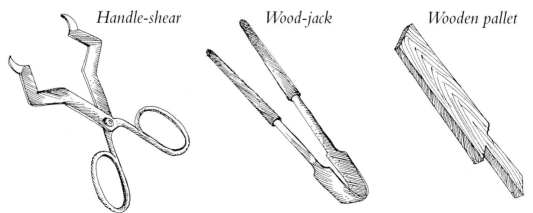

Handle-shear *Wood-jack* *Wooden pallet*

Steuben has been making glass in Steuben County in Corning, New York for a very long time. The county was given the name Steuben to honor Baron Von Steuben, General George Washington's drillmaster, who was sent to Valley Forge during the American Revolution to reorganize the Continental army in the terrible winter of 1777-1778. The residents and glassmakers since that time have changed the pronunciation of the name to *Stoo-ben*, with the accent on the last syllable, and that is how the name is said today.

The red-hot furnaces were roaring like a herd of walruses. I stood before one of them, clutching my drawings. I felt small as a piece of butter beginning to melt. The foreman introduced me to the gaffer Sammy Carlinio, head of a four-man shop. Sammy smiled at me as kindly as an Inuit hunter, and lent me a cup to get some coffee.

"What are we going to make?" Sammy asked as I shook hands with the other three members of our shop: the servitor, the bit gatherer, and the stick-up boy. They all looked carefully at my design of a polar bear.

"I picked this bear first because it should be easy," I told them.

"May be hard," Sammy groaned. "Call up two and a half minutes of glass," he yelled to our servitor, who hurried back to us with a fiery slug of red-hot glass on the end of a pontil iron almost as tall as Sammy.

Sammy quickly thrust into the roaring glory hole the glass slug on the end of the iron and started turning it, reheating it while singing an aria from the opera *Carmen*.

The polar bear drawn on paper looked easy to make, but proved difficult. While we tried to shape the bear's body, its head grew too hot and drooped like a melting icicle. While we tried to shape the bear's legs, its tail end grew cold. Then, like an ice cube out of the refrigerator, it cracked, blew off the iron, and smashed onto the floor. I was worried.

"Let's try your dinosaur drawing," Sammy said. "It may be easier to make."

We called for a big new slug of glass. It was soft. Sammy started swinging the glass around like a drum major leading a band, then swung more slowly until the dinosaur's body stretched. Sammy reheated the glass while our bit gatherer brought us four large bits. Each bit was shaped into a leg and stuck on. He brought a smaller bit for the head. Finally, using a wet paddle, I curved the neck and tail, making the dinosaur look alive. As the glass began to cool, Sammy cracked the dinosaur off the iron. The carry-in boy caught it in his heatproof mittens and put it in the kiln.

The story of King Arthur pulling the magic sword, Excalibur, out of the stone has always excited me. It sounds easy, doesn't it, to plunge a small metal blade into a pool of hot glass, leaving a perfect hole in the ice-hard crystal? Trying that was my greatest challenge.

Leonard Parker was the gaffer when we made *Excalibur*. At first, it was like sticking a spoon in a pot of honey. The hot glass sagged down with the sword. We tried a hundred times – day shifts, night shifts – and still we failed. We were about to give up when an old retired glassmaker asked what I was trying to do. When I told him, he shook his head. "You'll never make it that way, son." He whispered a secret in my ear.

Without much hope, we tried his suggestion. It worked like magic. We had learned how to plunge the sword blade into the soft glass and draw it out before it turned as hard as ice. I made sure the old man got a cash award for his idea.

"How do you do that Excalibur trick?" many glassmakers ask. But that's a special secret I'll never tell.

A wise goldsmith taught me to use hard wax and sculpt animal and human figures. I tried to make them with the same strength and beauty found in the stone carvings of Inuit/Eskimo hunters. I took these small sculptures to him to be cast. When he was finished, my wax had melted and been lost, replaced by gold or silver. I could hardly wait to affix the 18 karat gold or sterling silver to the glass, and examine the finished piece in a proper light. I was thrilled to see clear crystal and precious metals shining so beautifully together.

One of the best moments in glass making is the excitement of waking up in the early morning and imagining the shape and details of the glass designs you hope to make. The success you have depends on working with a really good gaffer and other persons in his shop.

I see white-hot glass as being almost alive and moving as it leaves the glory hole on the end of a blowing iron. It has always been a thrill for me to see it blown, to watch fire turn into ice after the sculpture has left the kiln and become a shining piece of crystal, like the unicorn that comes leaping mysteriously into your mind.

Clear glass seems to possess the magic of a crystal ball with all its strange shapes ever changing in the light, sometimes hiding, sometimes reflecting wonderful rainbow colors.

I like to make glass that tells its own story without using words. You only need to look at *Elf and Mushroom* to imagine that it reflects a famous poem from earlier times. *Rip Van Winkle*, *Excalibur*, and *Unicorn* also cause you to remember old myths and legends. I've yet to make *The Goose that Laid the Golden Egg*, but I intend to.

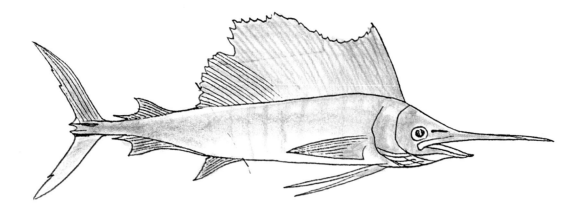

When making *Trout and Fly*, Parker was eager to be the gaffer, for we both loved fishing. After looking at the drawings, we decided to make some big bubbles in the glass like spots on a trout.

"Call up enough hot glass," I said.

After the bubbles were inside the oval-shaped body, Parker reheated the glass in the glory hole and swung it until it was the right length. Then with strong scissors, he cut the hot glass tail into shape, and I bent the fish into a lively leap. I marked the hot glass with chalk, and Parker put on eyes and fins. Then he cut open the mouth and blew air inside to shape it.

"It's finished," I declared, and the carry-in boy put on his thick mittens.

Parker cracked the trout off the iron. Its bubbles shone like diamonds as it was carried to cool in the kiln. Our shop continued making trout for several days. When they were cool, we lined them up. I picked the best one, then I hooked my favorite golden fly into its mouth. We broke all the other fish into the cullet barrel, and I hand-carried this best trout to New York.

Making pencil drawings from nature has often led me to creating some new designs in glass. It is like looking through a window into the secret world where wild animals live.

Among my favorite birds are the elegant, long-legged cranes and herons. The cranes, like wild geese, make long flights north and south, wintering in Texas or Mexico, and nesting in Canada's north in spring. These cranes, wearing their bright, red-feathered helmets, are as tall as many girls or boys. The strange calls of the cranes can be heard a long way off. When they meet, they face each other. They spread their wings and leap into the air, then come gracefully floating back to earth to bow politely, and repeat this dance again.

I've watched these cranes year after year near the Alaskan–Canadian border. They dance at dawn and in the evening light under a rising moon. Beneath that same moon, you can sometimes hear the lonesome singing of wolves or coyotes – a sound that makes you shiver when you hear it through the mountains or across the plains.

We sailed north one summer along the wonderfully rugged coastline of Norway, where Lapps herd reindeer, and night owls hunt through the dark forest. We sailed to Bear Island and to the northernmost islands of Svalbard. The sky at midnight over those high Arctic islands was as bright as at noonday. We watched whales spouting great clouds of white steam into the clear, bright, summer night. The icebergs clustering near our ship lit my imagination and made me start drawing whole parades of crystal sculptures.

Returning to the Arctic has always given me new ideas. And the Inuit/Eskimo people have made it seem like going home.

Traveling in wild parts of the world gives me a thrill. To write or make drawings about any place takes only a pad of paper, colored pencils, and a pen.

Some winters I go to Florida to watch dolphins feeding and playing in the blue-green ocean. I have made many drawings of these wonderful creatures. I modeled them – half in, half out – diving into a solid block of crystal, their silver tails shining in the air above.

When I was nine or ten and a young art student studying at the Art Gallery of Ontario, my art teacher, Dr. Arthur Lismer, made a journey to Africa. After many months, he returned home. We were all excited! Suddenly, the sound of African drums and singing could be heard through the galleries. A tall thin dancer wearing a huge Ashanti mask appeared. "It's Dr. Lismer!" we cried out. "He's back!" We all started to shout and skip and sing. I could imagine this famous artist teacher of mine paddling up the Congo River in a dugout canoe with huge crocodiles swimming all around him, and lions and leopards following him through the jungle and along the riverbanks.

At that very moment, I made up my mind to go to Africa and to all the other wild, faraway places in the world. In 1974, I went on safari to East Africa – to Kenya and Tanzania – famous for herds of elephants and zebras, fleet-footed gazelles, and prides of lions, leopards, and rhinoceroses; so many different kinds of birds, hippopotamuses, and crocodiles. There I saw the snow-topped mountain of Kilimanjaro, and the great flat plains with tall giraffes, wildebeests, and swift cheetahs; sights I'll never forget in all my life. I filled my sketchbooks with hundreds of drawings, some of which have turned into glass designs. The Masai were there as well – tall, thin, elegant, cattle-herders – a unique people in a truly awesome land.

Green Heron is one of my most recent glass designs. It requires a lot of skillful, copper-wheel engraving by an expert. It also has a golden feather. I am fascinated by the fact that this small, graceful heron is one of the very few tool-using animals or birds.

It has recently been discovered that the green heron (common on both coasts of North America) has an amazing fly-fishing technique. This shy bird plucks a tiny under feather from its own breast, and places it on the water to attract small fish. When a fish comes to the green heron's lure, the bird, with a slightly open beak, strikes the fish with a lightning-quick thrust timed at less than half a second.

In making *Blue Whale*, I searched for the right feeling, designing a tall glass form that would show the great depths of the ocean. I planned this piece so it would be frosted white on top to look like waves or polar ice. The blue whale is the largest creature that has ever lived in this world, and is much larger than the dinosaurs. I portrayed this huge, air-breathing animal diving and alone, for not many are still alive today.

And what of the sound of glass? It is so like the sound of candle ice in the Arctic giving off one of the purest, clearest sounds in nature. This happens only in early summer when the snow has melted on top of an ice-covered lake. First, blue reflecting pools of water form, then slowly cracks appear, and candlelike shapes occur in the ice. Thousands of these pieces of ice remain floating upright in the water.

In summer I used to go to a lake called Tassiujakjuak, when it was frozen, and pitch my tent on a small island just for the pleasure of hearing this ice moved by the evening breeze. The icy candles began slowly collapsing against one another, giving off a delicate tinkling sound like that of the finest crystal glasses held by their stems and touched together.

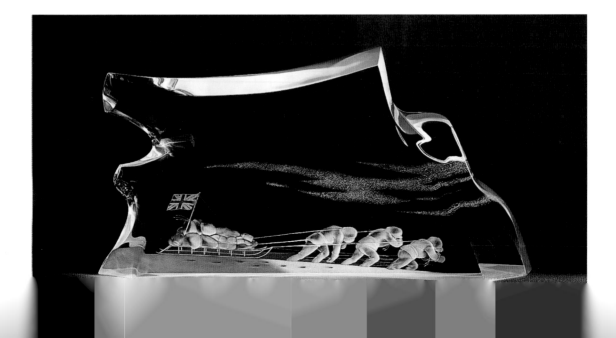

Photographs of Houston sculptures courtesy Steuben

Drawings by James Houston